- rallying against sexual assault and harassment

a women's poetry anthology

Edited by Deborah Alma

Fair Acre Press

Published by Fair Acre Press in 2018
www.fairacrepress.co.uk

Anthology copyright © 2018 by Deborah Alma

Printed and bound by Lightning Source
Lightning Source has received Chain of Custody (CoC) certification from:
The Forest Stewardship Council™ (FSC®)
Programme for the Endorsement of Forest Certification™ (PEFC™)
The Sustainable Forestry Initiative® (SFI®).

A CIP catalogue record for this title is available from the British Library.

ISBN 978-1-911048-29-9

Cover design by Sandra Salter www.saltysstudio.com

Ink drawings by Jessamy Hawke www.jessamyhawke.co.uk

Contents

Part One   'silly lasses'

Part Two   'my ordinary walk home'

Part Three   'I see myself lie quiet as snow on rail tracks'

Part Four   'Domestic'

Part Five 'They can't help it'

Part Six 'I said I was the proof'

Part Seven   'make for the light'

Foreword

The global primal scream of #MeToo helped the silent find their voices. We created a new solidarity through language. #MeToo was about us finding the words, finding their order and stringing them together. Finally our words mattered and people listened.

This collection of poems beautifully celebrates this new language. A collection that ranges from sad hidden truths hoping to tell their secret quietly, to big defiant two fingers up to the years of knowing that we all just put up with the touching, the power and the game. The tone and styles are different but the story is universal.

I worked for years at Women's Aid with women who had been abused. I have worked with women imprisoned by their secrets, women who were bought and sold, young girls told to keep the secret by the man everyone else trusted. It all begins with a power imbalance that keeps women quiet and in their place. It is hard to express how tired years of feminist activism can make a person. Many times when sexual violence court cases fell through and no further action was taken, or a girl told us of how the boys at school passed her around; I felt that I was hitting a brick wall. It can feel that there is very little hope.

#MeToo is that hope. Something changed and two small words spoke a million stories. Women have few advantages over our male brethren but one we do have is sisterhood. Our sisterhood makes us want to stand together, it makes us feel the pain of another on a familiar path. Our sisterhood created #MeToo and it was in the comfort of someone else's bravery, nudging us to pass it on. I have seen breakthroughs in women's liberation before, small steps in the right direction; a law change here and woman elected there, but #MeToo feels different. It feels as if it came from us together, not asking for something but instead demanding it. I feel as if we might be winning the argument.

It may seem only like a small act of defiance to make an indelible mark write a poem or draw up a banner to march with, but there is posterity in an image and in this book. This is an artifact of a time when things were changing. I dream of an era when young people read these tales with disbelief and shock as my children do about segregation or men being imprisoned for their sexuality. For now they will stay a defiant reality.

With each and every poet in this collective I say #metoo.

Jess Phillips
January 2018

Introduction

This book came straight out of a long thread on my Facebook page in October 2017. I asked women friends of mine to add their name to the thread if they hadn't experienced any form of sexual harassment in their lives and I was surprised to find that of the 200 women that started to share some of their stories, 2 or 3 said that it had never happened to them. My surprise was not that there were so few, but that there were any women at all. Take a look at Gill Lambert's poem *It Didn't Mean Me*: this happened to one woman on the thread who changed her mind when she thought about it.

These #MeToo conversations started all over social media in the wake of the Harvey Weinstein allegations, as we listened to male news reporters being genuinely shocked when they asked women if they'd ever experienced anything similar, and being told 'Of course' and 'Yes, many times' and 'Every woman'.

We have shared these stories over and over with our friends, sisters, mothers, partners and sometimes with the police, or in court. It has been the water we swim in as women. But saying something publically has always been difficult and brave. The words stick in our throats, for so many reasons.

Something was released and given a space within social media. It was easy to add our voice to the rising shout of #MeToo. We felt the sisterhood. Many women felt emboldened by this to share more difficult stories, more details; the lid has come off this box and now cannot be forced back on.

I'm a poet, and an editor, and someone suggested we collect these stories somehow and it was obvious to collect them as poems. It was what I could do.

I am very proud of this book, proud of the poets for sharing their stories and for putting their names to their words. It is a painful and difficult read a great deal of the time, I get that. Take it slowly, read only what you can bear. I hope that the reader will hear its rallying cry of anger and impatience, its strong message that we have had enough.

And to the men who speak up with us and for us, I hope, as the essayist Rebecca Solnit says*, that they will 'understand that feminism is not a scheme to deprive men but a campaign to liberate us all'.

The final section of the book deals with a coming back to the light; they are poems of recovery and strength out of some very dark places. There are beautiful, peaceful poems that reach out to other women and, as Roz Goddard says in her poem *This Poem is For You*, the book, I hope, is other women

> gathering me in boat arms
>
> attending there, as one dawn
> gave way to another, until I was strong.

Deborah Alma
January 2018

P.S. At the time of going to press in the UK there are government proposals that would remove funding for short-term supported housing from the welfare system. This would have a devastating effect on refuges, with Women's Aid warning that four in every ten refuges would have to close. This housing benefit accounts for 53% of their funding.

Years ago I was unlucky enough to be in an abusive relationship. I had an emergency bag packed for me and my children hidden at the back of a cupboard and a Women's Aid phone number ready in my phone... I never used them, but my god they made all the difference, knowing that they were there. All the proceeds in this book will go to Women's Aid to help them fight to keep these refuges open.

I have been asked to share a poem of my own, so that #MeToo is me too.

* Rebecca Solnit - Men Explain Things to Me (Granta Books, 2014)

for my sons, Joe Alma and Hayden Kitson
I am very proud of you.

Part One

'silly lasses'

Reeds

This is 1988. A disused
quarry   the pits
a mix of chalk and shale
now filled with green water
geese and ducks. Men fish here.

Two wild ten year olds
at the edge strip
to cozzies   underneath
their shorts   dip in. the water
like brain freeze

becomes the norm.   rocks
are sharp as kitten teeth. reeds
soft fingers   the green/blue beautiful
the sun is a thumb print.   one
dips underneath.   the other
is on the shore   drying herself

pulling on shorts over thin
white goose bumped legs,
while the men watch and fish.

Wendy Pratt

Nervous

It's just a game
that girls and boys from school play in the park.

They move a hand
slowly up one of your legs.

You make your mind a strong
blank calico sail.

Their soft hand touches your shin,
knee, thigh.

You try to stare at the horizon.

Your skin is mottled
a bit purple by the wind.

When you can't tolerate it any longer
you say
nervous
and they stop.

The girl who tolerates it the longest
is the winner.

That's how you win the game.
You just have to tolerate it.

Sally Jenkinson

Sometime before Myra*

Even now I wonder, was I right about him,
the man who asked us if we'd like to see his rabbits?
I'd heard whispers of kids being 'interfered with'.

The older girl, minding me, wanted to go with him
but I knew wild rabbits wouldn't wait for us
and who takes a hutch on to waste ground at night?

I was wrapped in a scarf of mother's fears,
with spells knitted tight against the dark,
and pinned to my vest was the holy scapular.

'Don't go with him! Run for the fair!'
Although *my mother said I never should
go with the gypsies*, it was only a rhyme.

We ran across the road to brassy lights:
the Wurlitzer, bobbing ducks, pink candy floss,
past the gun range, looking for a stranger to trust.

Men had urges, couldn't help themselves.
Our mums said a woman could never hurt us,
though we should never get into anyone's car.

The dodgem woman hurried us to church.
She rang the priest's bell, gabbled our story.
Our mothers cried when they came to collect us.

Walking home past waste-ground newly fenced
where he said his rabbits lived, I'd see,
through wire mesh, an orange plastic ball.

Angela Topping

Myra Hindley helped Ian Brady, the Moors Murderer, to procure his victims.

Stages of Child Abuse

I'm afraid of the three witches in Macbeth
God and the Sisters of Mercy and death.
I'm afraid of breaking the Commandments.
The Sisters of Mercy want to know
Why were you not in mass child?

The man with stained teeth buys me sweets
asks, *why are you crying pet?*
Mammy tells me to be careful of dirty old men.
I scratch the backs of my knees until they bleed.
The priest makes the sign of the cross
on my forehead, with a thumb of ash.
In the name of the Father, the Son and the Holy Ghost.

Mammy tells me stories of hospitals,
of angry matrons that strapped her to the chair
and force fed her mince and gravy pie.
She tells me when she was a little girl
her mammy sent her to play with the boy next door
who made her lie down and do things on the cold, dirty lino.

Every night I can't sleep.
I twist myself into knots between starched sheets
and try to think of good things.
But I dream of death
blood stains my hands crimson red.

When I wake, I see rosary beads
the five sorrowful mysteries, and the Sisters of Mercy
gold rings gleaming on their knuckled fingers.
Tap, tap, tap, as they try to get inside my head.

Rachel Burns

Undone

We had to run for the bus after confession,
where waiting for Mother's silence
I'd made imaginary idols of saints, illuminated

by twenty votives I paid for with flickers
of prayer. We'd no time for my litany
of lies and spite and rage so the priest winked

and told me *Next time*. I reached for Mother's
hand, already crammed with beads
clacking together: a metronome for OCD.

Her illness worshipped muttering; stations
of the cross mostly, but then anything
with a repeating pattern, lost in a hail of Marys.

She let me sit by the window, while, head
bowed she vowed to settle breaths above
the throb and grind of engine. Her hands knitted

together then apart, twisting and fidgeting inside
deliberate sleeves. She looked as odd
as the panting man in the soiled mac, uncurtaining

bushes when we stopped at lights. He grinned
up at me, presenting his puffy, purpley
grub. I covered up my eyes and whispered:

How soon is next time Mummy?   *Mum?*

Kaddy Benyon

Dog

At first, he seems nice.
Just a man with a beard, walking his dog -
only there is no dog and there is a wood
and the dog has run off and
could we help him find it, please?
My cousin is seven, with fizzy red hair
and she says, *yeah, okay, what's he called?*
Rex, he says, after a really long time
and I think, *no, we mustn't go*
into the wood to look for that dog
and I am eight and oldest
so I say, *no, I don't think so* - and he says,
have you seen one of these?
His jeans are undone and he's pulling
and I say *yeah, sure, my dad has one*
but it isn't as big and he pulls harder and says,
would you like to touch it? and I say,
No way! so he grabs my wrist and his face twists
and it burns and the voice in my head
that sounds a lot like Mum, shouts *RUN!*
and we run, so fast my heart is thumping
and I'm shouting at my cousin *hurry up!*
and she stops and says,

but what about the dog?

Victoria Bennett

Between Us

Separating our gardens was the breeze-block
wall patterned with a hollowed-out
flower. Before it threw me, I straddled
that rough horse, half on home-ground
and squashed red velvet mites so it looked like

I had been bloodied in battle.
Soon enough I fell for it - the other side,
because of the swing and brand-new paddling pool.
Surely, I ignored the terrible shed
with its stare of a window, the vice
on the work-table, and jaw-open door? No
amount of swinging over a lattice of roses,
carefully tended could let me unsee what I saw.

clare e. potter

Parental Guidance

Think now of the young girl
in her pink room
who still owns a bear
a book of princesses
staring into the mirror
through the eyes
of a camera

into a world she
does not yet know
or fully understand
she is over young yet
does not know what
it is to be a woman
how those men
will see her.

They will blame her lips
her breasts barely risen.
They will blame her long legs
in white lace socks
say Sunday sandals
smoothed by baby hands
made them look down.

Someone's daughter;
Oh, that I must tell her this...

Sue Hardy-Dawson

To the Giant Ground Sloth in the Natural History Museum

You surprised me, lurking in a gallery
of framed plesiosaurs and ichthyosaurs –
those fossils like fish bones on tinfoil
– but pleasantly; not like the stranger
in a stained tracksuit who flashed his cock
in an underpass when I was fourteen.
They've given you a tree to embrace.
It's branchless; you caress its smooth bark
between broad claws and stumpy legs
cast in plaster under Victorian arches.
Evolution shrank you, reduced you, forced
you to climb trees you once stood eye-high to.
Evolution exhausted you. His shadow
rests on bricks the shade of old urinals.

Natalie Whittaker

Travelling

November midnight, a village somewhere
on the Rhône. I am twenty, so is she.
And we are broke.

In a shut-down campsite
we lie
in sleeping bags

and listen to their breath,
their footsteps,
circling the tent.

We unfold our new penknives
mean
to use them.

Except
that silence falls
again.

We shake. We curse them all,
mean
every word.

Jean Atkin

Giantess

They have been teaching boys
to be scared of us getting bigger.

Whispering in their ears
that they should shout us down
if they catch us
trying to stretch and strengthen our legs.

Creep up on us
if they find the hiding places
where we go to tense our muscles,
or eat.

Photograph us eating on the underground
or failing that
straight up our skirts.

Laugh if they catch us in a power stance,
expanding, with nothing to fear.

Sally Jenkinson

Fidget

It's the summer holidays and here I am fidgety
at fourteen, taking a factory job and fidgeting
money away on make-up, my fingers fidgeting
over poultry-farm chickens – how they fidget
even after they're dead. Their guts fidget
their way into a slop trough, their smell fidgets
up my nostrils. The conveyer belt fidgets
and creates defects: feather-stubs fidget
on torn lips of skin. I'm told to work faster. I fidget
harder with gloves that are always a fidget
to get on and off. I watch the older women fidget
to tie twine below their knees so the rats won't fidget
up their trousers. The clock-in clock fidgets
its way forward somehow and the foreman fidgets
with his boiler-suit buttons and because everyone's fidgeted
off to work by now, tells me to fidget
with the fidgety thing he holds in his hands.

Elisabeth Sennitt Clough

In the self-defence class

we were taught to block, side hand to temple
elbow to chest, run as fast as you can.
If grabbed by the waist pull
both thumbs hard!

It probably helped, the day
an attacker grabbed from behind
swung me round to force a kiss.
My hand hit his temple, lucky blow.

I ran.
          My fitness at nineteen mattered.

But it was late
late for the girl at seven
molested by a neighbour, late
for the unwary eleven year old

when a different instructor
was hell bent on simulating
sex attacks on two young girls

using his tall lean frame
to hold us down   my friend
sent for fitness training
after a breakdown.

Words console, never enough.

A cello chord
unpicks
          ancient scabs.

Rona Fitzgerald

Interval ice-cream

Four bows float in the stage light.
We will return to our bodies
when the fiery air quietens
and the leader smiles sideways,
slowly lowering his arm.

We will hurt our hands and shout.
The stage flowers will shiver
as the players walk away.
Music feeds the soul,
it feeds the soul.

The interval ice cream girl
has raspberry lips, vanilla
skin and a dark stain on the
left hand side of her neck:
the love bite of a violin.

The one who flourished his bow
in triumph like a spear,
who stares out darkly
from the posters, he loves
raspberry and vanilla.

If she's over sixteen, he'll offer
a special rate; be encouraging.
She will learn so much, so fast.
Music feeds the soul,
it feeds the soul.

Sarah Mnatzaganian

Silly Lasses

for Isabel, Dundee 1975

We'd been down the baths
for our after-work wash
and walked the wet streets
pink and laughing,
going home
to our tenement flat,
red lanterns at the window,
full-volume 'It's All Right Now' -

to be woken in the small hours
by muttering at the door,
low and murderous, a man
worrying the lock
trying to get in. Blood-cold
we pushed a bedside cabinet, chair, hoover
up against the door.
No mobiles then, no landline,
no way out but the landing
where he was crouched
murmuring and cursing.
The door gave slightly
but held until, eventually
footsteps on the stair,
a long silence.
First light we ran together to the phone box, called the police.
On the jute mat he'd left two ropes, each neatly coiled
and knotted into a noose.

The constable looked at us.
'What d'you expect, silly lasses, with your red bulbs
and hippy signs on the door?' Under his breath,
I almost imagined it, he added *'hoors'*.

Pippa Little

Part Two

'my ordinary walk home'

The landmarks change when you walk home

Tuck your hair and scarf under your jacket and zip it
so it can't get grabbed. Why did you bring a bag?
Don't you have pockets? Hold your keys in your hand.
Can you run in those heels? Should've worn jeans.
Play a brisk walking rhythm in your head, something edgy
and noisy and hope the mood is reflected in your expression.
There's the "Cheer Up Love, It Might Never Happen" Spot.
Here's the "It's Your Lucky Night" Clock Tower -
an offer I didn't take up. Here's the Avoid At All Costs
Underpass, even if you have to wait for the light to go red.
Here's the Please Keep Your Eyes On The Road
Railway Bridge. It ends at Wolf-whistle Stretch, but keep
your speed constant. You can't rest if you get out
of breath. Don't wait if a car approaches the junction
you have to cross, walk further along, cross further
down and walk back. Repeat as often as necessary.
I know it adds to the journey but think of the extra
calories burned. Here's Polo Road where four buddies
wanted the birthday boy to lose his virginity. I figured
I could make the dead end before them and hoped
they wouldn't get out and run after me. Here's Number
Eleven - the age of the boy who asked for sex, who was bigger
and heavier despite his age. Go past Proposition Lamppost.
I don't think I need to explain, do I? Don't look. Keep up.
That day I stupidly wore those clacky heels, this is Talk
To Yourself Loudly Street, where I hoped the two men
who'd already seen me wouldn't be interested in a mad woman.
This is News Corner where nipping out for a Sunday paper
in paint-splattered clothes won me a suitor with a wedding
ring willing to pay. I said no, obvs. Skip That Street: among
the run down, MOT-failures, a silver Mercedes was found,
owner the boot, her throat garroted. She had a wedding ring
too. You're slowing, keep up, not far now. Unless that family
saloon circles again. I was about to Turn To My Front Door
when the driver asked how much. I told him he only
drove a Ford and he sped off. But I still had to walk round

the block to make sure he didn't know I lived here
on my ordinary street at the end of my ordinary walk home.

Emma Lee

Scold's Bridle

Such a Bridle for the tongue, as not only quite deprives [women] of
speech but brings shame for the transgression and humility thereupon
. . .   Encyclopædia Metropolitana (1845)

drive your iron tongue into my mouth
                    fell me of my speaking
              ride me through the streets   dumb beast
        this carnival   of spitting, pissing
              you think it makes a manful man of you?

the root of me is driven down to silence
                              to some dark earth
anchoress
        my tongue is pricked and raw
              god's words are kindling in my throat

Helen Ivory

After Eden

My birth day came with a fall
of spring snow, those restless flakes,
unable to settle in the pulse
of a nascent earth, a dove
in the flagged yard, fussing
over scattered grain, broadcasting
kernels like myths into the cracks
of legend.

Daughter of Eve, I'm bred
for domesticity, conditioned
to home. Given a ring to distinguish me,
I learned the cramp of being woman,
lofty mother, builder of nests.

Sometimes, I fancy I've never known
this lumbering frame, its slavish attraction
to earthiness. My impulse throbs
in the bloom of the dove's breast,
yet it seems, no matter how wholesome
the flesh, there's always a grubby
worm that eats away at the core.

'Whore,' they call me, if I strut my stuff,
puff out my breasts, sing too loudly,
so I mapped the skies,
navigated the small lives of men,
through the compass of her eye,
the homeliness of her nature.

It's the need of my flesh that keeps me
returning to my niche. Released,
I'd beat my angel wings,
let the restless feathers fall,
watch them settle like snow on the garden,
vaned messages of a spirit set free.

Stella Wulf

Robosexual

Honey™ is the perfect woman
to fulfill your every fantasy!
Built to your exact requirements,
Honey™ is available in a variety
of skin tones, with changeable hair
and her own special selection of outfits
or , if you prefer, her birthday suit!
Honey™ has a unique, real-feel vagina
in the softest silicone, with a refillable
squirt unit for mega-moist climaxes.
Honey™ comes with pre-loaded phrases
and authentic screams* of pain and ecstasy.
Honey™ has fully poseable limbs,
internal shock absorbers and patented
strike zones for punching and kicking.
Honey™ never argues, nags or refuses,
you can drop this girl down the stairs
and she'll thank you afterwards!
With a detachable head for decapitation play
and strong, permanent bondage points
to limbs and neck for all your hog-tie needs,
however dark your fantasies and desires
Honey™ is the only woman you'll ever want!

*battery not included
Clare Hill

Second Person Personal

It must have been around dusk
when you were strolling home
the last half mile from the tube
along empty Willesden streets
the plane trees glowing green
with a blackbird mistaking
the street lights for day
and singing loudly above you
that you think
you are being followed
and you pick up speed
but the stalker shuffles his feet
too close behind you
so you swing round and shout at him
you should know better
and *how dare you*
and *I know where you live*
you bastard!

Meg Cox

The Bestiary

after Guillaume Apollinaire

Zeus

Here you are again, eyeing
your latest prize. Such a ladies' man,
such appetites, always taking
what you crave. So mighty, controlling
the skies, prowling the city,
lightning bolt ready to strike.

The colleague

He hasn't yet mastered transformation
into a swan or a shower of gold
but the eye works double-time:
across the table, in the hallway.
Unless it's just some minor irritation,
a fleck of corporate dust.

The sportsman

So serious, wearing his all-business gear
behind his important-man desk,
thundering questions of education and
ambition. At night, his voice on the line,
slithering that most cliché of queries:
What are you wearing right now?

The masseur

She's alone in the park, reading, just
reading when the stranger's fingers
begin kneading her neck, the palms
spreading to the shoulders as she
bounds to her feet — How does she
know him? Surely she must?

The seeker

There's safety in numbers. Or so
you think until you find him
behind you, his hand slipping
between you and your friend,
twisting to find its perfect fit
at the front of your skirt.

The god on the train

There is no safety in numbers, rush hour
bodies crammed so tight, it's a cinch
for him to wiggle his hips into you,
grind as the train sways and you
throw an elbow straight to his gut
*Oh, I'm so sorry. Won't you please
excuse me?*

Michelle Penn

Just One Example

Then there's that other arsehole:
Mr I-Wouldn't-Touch-You-With-A-Bargepole
Mr You're-Not-My-Type-At-All
Add any of: too fat, too loud, too small
Funny that (I'd want to say)
When seconds ago you'd grabbed my arm, blocked my way
But I don't speak it – I let it stand
Keys threaded carefully through my hand
Walking late – a pedestrian gladiator
With my armoured finger separator
It was just so tiresome to have to do
Me Too. Me Too. Me Too

Jemima Laing

Bitch

Always just within reach, it is the desk-drawer revolver
or the switch that is flicked when a woman says No
and means No and knows her own mind
and makes herself inconveniently clear;

it is the cocksure roar of boy used to his own way,
one more of the ones we warn each other about,
whose reputations we pass around like classroom
secrets, names itching from girl-hand to woman-hand,

the ones who *just adore women*, who say their wives
really don't mind, the ones who wonder, aloud,
and publicly, what hitch qualifies *you* to claim
this space for your small fierce self,

the ones who will scrape back their chair, stand up
in the kitsch restaurant, tongue catching on the latch
of that single syllable, the alarmed door he will shoulder
open becoming the exit she will depart through.

Jane Commane

Enough

14
a lift to the loganberry field
just us 3
the gear shifts as his fingers slip from the stick
to my knee

16
a passing car slows
we want it
we're fit
my sister spits
we're ugly bitches

18
a shared student house
our landlord keeps a key
7am   he lets himself in
it *is* his house
he's just being friendly

19
we grow accustomed to the stranger
draw the curtains when we see him
his back towards us in our yard
it's almost funny
except when I'm alone

20
my *no* laughed off
I feign sleep
dead prey is normally ignored
8 hours until he leaves
and I can breathe

24
ground floor flat
a face at the window
no phone
no back door
we sit in silence
wait until light

28
I pick up pace in the dark
he follows my lead
I dart across the road
he follows my lead
I sprint to my front gate
up the path to my front door
hear the gate clank closed behind him
I'm in
safe   for now

41
sunny seclusion
circular stone windbreak offers protection
from Tenerife breeze
but not from prying eyes
he stands
hands down trunks
watches as I race to dress
and leave his beach

46
fortunate
all my stories small
but always wary
and always wondering
whether they are enough
for me to say
me too

Amy Rainbow

I Have Been A Long Time Without Thinking

The mind as an empty and flooded field.
The mind as water that rises up through the green.
The mind as the tree at the edge of the field.

I have been a long time without thinking.
White birds with no names.
They row away through the air.

I have been a long time without thoughts of my own.
They built a fence round the field.
They named the trees and the birds.

They built this train and the line that runs past.
They told me to walk up and down.
If I did it they cheered.

I am reading in the place that they built.
Adrienne Rich said *read as if your life depended on it.*
A man asks me what I'm reading.

He tells me about his job and his wife and his children.
I put my book away. Repeat. Repeat. I put my book away.
He tells me about money and Brexit and immigration.

I have been putting my book away all my life.
I put away my hands and my mouth and my eyes.
I can sit here and listen and live without field or water or green.

Or go back and fold into myself.
Or enter the field and drink at the flooded place.
Or enter and prepare to be followed. Or not.

I am worried that they made the field.
Maybe they gave me the water.
I am worried about madness and the next sixty seconds.

I put away my heart and the stillness inside.
I smile and say so what do you do tell me again and
how many kids do you have remind me again of your wife

Kim Moore

Exile

Love as a yes to the world
is difficult when I am
besieged by fingers and thighs
and strong strangling arms.

I am bedraggled by the touch
of desire without invite
and I can choose to stay here
in full body armour,

hard-eyed, light guttering,
here where pleasures are
but at a price, or I can
unpack my boots and go,

with a map and a plan
and a bag of good books
to where hills and sky and
sea collide unseen,

go to where snow falls
untouched but for where
my feet tread.
And yet, to stand alone

under endless steely sky –
what use inner light then
if there is no one,
no one for miles, to see?

Rachel Buchanan

It Didn't Mean Me

I didn't think it meant me. I'd never
felt a flat blade on my face, knuckle crack
against bone, an open-palm slap.

I'd never run from a shadow-traced
pavement, gone home to shower
him out of me, stripped for a copper.

I'd not flinched or positioned myself
out of reach, not curled, turned
inside-out with the fear of certainty.

I've not felt the cold prick of brick
on my back, a door shutting out safety,
or had bruises I'd have to explain.

But I've felt his hand on my leg as his wife
drove us home. His breath on my ear,
proprietorial fingers, stronger than mine.

A zip going down, an unbuckling belt,
a head full of dates and unwanted babies,
a slack mouth and his tongue stealing

kisses that weren't his to take.
My legs crossed against him, my body
jammed shut and still, *still* letting him in.

I didn't think it meant me,
when you said what had happened to you.
But actually yeah, me too.

Gill Lambert

Tumescence Inflammatoria

The ingenuity of his bend-down gambit
was the routine nature of a medical test, though
unforeseen from a psychologist.
Recounting his major achievements he
ushered me into the buff-walled room
and positioned behind me took
a hold of my wrist to measure my heartbeat
during the rigorous bending and standing and bending
and standing to the pace of his count.
As his rhythm reached a crescendo he pressed
my palm to the ruck of his trousers, hard
as a carapace. Last I recall, aconite
flowers were lacing his sill: poison-tips arrowing
over the casing, a pistil's flick from his tea.

Vasiliki Albedo

An Ancient Settlement

This is a true story, though I cannot believe it now.
We travelled in the black Mercedes,
and maybe, like me, you'll want to know where, and how.
I wore a blue skirt and I wore a white blouse –
this I recall because I wore them for seven days.

That first day, I did not mind.
When we stopped off, I thought we were nowhere.
And though afterwards we got back into the car,
and drove to the house where I was held,
and though after two days I was bored,
and though by the fourth I'd raised my fist
against his pinching of my cheek,
against his thick thigh,
his thick hand resting on my blue skirt,
I do not regret the journey.

This may surprise you.

For when we stopped that first late afternoon,
I turned the corner into the reddening sun.
Before me lay stones, and stones on stones:
some half-tumbled into low walls,
some etched with chariots and geometric vines,
some worked into columns supporting the sky,
some lying loose and heavy in the grass.
Through the lintel-less gateway of towering sphinxes
I saw round-breasted goddesses
eyeing the fluting god-processions
from behind their untamed, stony hair.

And so later, when he turned to face me,
and when later still he cursed my name,
above his rage I heard those ancient voices,
heard them rise, stride out free and wild,
into the singing grasslands of the night.

Liz Lefroy

Part Three

'I see myself lie quiet as snow on rail tracks'

Fireweed

They like disturbed ground
said someone then
when she was small
and in love with trains

for she was a rosebay willow-herb spotter
and the mystery of tunnels
was of dying men
perspiring
                           to tear deep-earth ragged
for fireweed to thrive on.

Now

they lie half-up
half-down the bank
                           if there are trains
                           she'll not be on them
taking languorous commuter stares
through smear-reflecting windows
to blink in quiet astonishment
the detail of a moment

Here on a siding
they are pressing down rosebay
and she is picking pink petals off
hot-prickled skin

All over in a minute,
he says; you have got to let go.

It is the rosebay she feels sorry for
damp, tissue-paper furls dropped

anyhow.

AM Hill

Sirens

The peeling lighthouse no longer functions:
the keeper evicted herself so long ago
there's no one here to remember the reason she left.
Whether after she was raped she left suddenly, in a moving strip of light
or gradually walked away along a shadow.

There are no lamps or lenses reflecting on rocks for vicious sailors,
no one to shine the beam, to warn of the dangers
of playing love songs on ship radios
over strange accompaniments, these thuds in the tides
and those wails of pulling, drowning gales.

Jess Richards

Easy target

I wait for the end of rape, for it to unhank blackness.
I see myself rope-ridden, body's dirt carelessly unravelled.

I see myself lie quiet as snow on rail tracks, slim-wristed,
the smell of spring in the air. I see myself crystallised,

gianted, knocked over and over until I disappear each day
knuckle-boned to his fist. I cannot win at this - wake

red-eyed each morning to dreams' unblinkedness.
I'm held out on a white tray, the misery of man's hands

at each rod of each rib like I'm rain wasting itself
in unrepaired guttering. Somewhere a remnant of me

spoors from long abandoned clothing,
fucking bleeds as if every vein is yanked from bone.

Abegail Morley

Dissecting Venus

*Morning Star, thy glory bright
far excels the sun's clear light.*
Moravian Carol

The robbers have removed their filthy selves
back to the boneyard
and now he is unchaperoned with her at last;
cuffs pristine as any welcome dinner guest,
eyes brimful of hunger.

The first cut seeps blood like Windsor soup.
He was expecting more.
But deeper in he swallows down
the pepper-green of myrtle.
Sea foam cleaves to his knife.

The dead girl holds up a copper mirror
to this tableau, and with her left hand
pulls back the drapery of her flesh
till the blinding light of heaven
falls to his grubby little room.

The spheres and the creatures of the zodiac
hurtle about his ears.
And as the dead girl rises up
she draws his lips to hers.
Too briefly, he divines he is the sun.

Helen Ivory

The Bicycle

I was OK   nothing had happened
nothing bad had happened
I couldn't get up from the bench
couldn't do up my dungarees
It was cold   it was night
The man had gone   and that was good
I was OK   I could sit up
peel myself from the bench's slats
which had pressed deep inside
It could have been worse
I was shaking   it was night
The bicycle was too heavy
My dungarees kept slipping
buttons were missing
I had to get home
It was so hard to walk
My head hurt   kept punching inside
my teeth couldn't stop talking
It could have been worse
My jaw hurt and my breasts were raw
I couldn't pick up the bicycle   its spinning wheel
couldn't walk with the bicycle
I had to get home   to wash
sleep   throw these clothes away
I was shaking   I was cold
My dungarees wouldn't do up
I would be alright   it was just
this bicycle   I needed

Katrina Naomi

scathless

no scars on me, lass
you said, walking away
and i could see clear, too
your enamelled composure, white
     flawless as a wedding night sheet
magic doors
in the mountainside closed over anything
i might have dared to say
beat
as i might at that unbroken surface
i am the child in the snow
stripped bare of argument and
shivering i revisit
the plain where new snow hides all
remembered footprints (and memory is not
to be trusted)

in the all
round white, hospital
white
     my mouth
     is full of snow

Mandy Macdonald

Skinned

In the corner, a boy peels my skin with a butter knife
while I watch from the door. He wants it to spiral
like orange peel. It falls like scales instead.

He rarely talks. He chooses instead to stab the air slow
and deliberately. This way he can be sure it registers.
I am meticulous with accounts. I know

the bottom line. He fingers my skin like a typewriter
whose keys are jammed, writes letters that lack
true eloquence. I cannot feel a thing.

Zelda Chappel

Secrets

She found a hiding place
in the shed by the disused train line,
tried out smoking,
played games on her mobile.

He watched her.
He wasn't going to do anything,
just talk.

I was at school with your brother.
He knows me.

She recognised him.
Carl. Curly blonde hair. Dark eyes.
Tall, like her brother,
scooter parked up by the fence.
He was nice. Listened.
Gave her fags. He was her secret.

He'd waited long enough,
forced her to lie on the striped rug
she'd smuggled from home,
gave her vodka with coke to loosen her up.
She spat it out.
Cost enough. Doesn't matter.

She never told anyone.
He got married a year or so after. Had kids.
She saw him sometimes
watching girls in the playground.

Cathy Whittaker

Undo

Unearthed
like something hiding
homeless
huddled from light.

Unclaimed
like the patch
by the skip
where everything spills.

Unwrapped
like a parcel of offal
slippery, coming
unstuck.

Unclothed
like an old cheese
blue veined
postdated.

Unskinned
like bruised fruit
fermented
honey and mud.

Unscrewed
at arms' length
full strength
and bitter.

Linda Goulden

My Fault

Consider my fault. It starts here,
on my temple so slim it could be a strand
of stray hair. Up close, at kissing distance,
it's bolder, a slip of charcoal eyeliner.

When I find it in the mirror, it moves,
the creeping leg of a spider, a crack
across a plate left in the oven too long.
It parts a fraction like the lips of someone

sleeping, breathing in an unfamiliar bed
and when I think of that, it widens,
crescent-shaped, smile of a moon
above the house they'd say I shouldn't

have been in, rim of the glass I shouldn't
have touched. It turns into a zip, slit
of a pencil skirt and I can feel my body
opening, a fault-line in the ground

and everything - his hands and books,
the quartered bread, the wine, the room
I don't remember entering - loosed
and falling into me. I turn

into a road that always takes me back
to the same place: pit town, midnight,
frost across the playing fields
as I go silent underneath

the broken roundabout, zig-zag
below pavements, terraces, the winding wheel
crossed with a thin seam of light and no-one
can touch me, not for centuries.

Helen Mort

Should I say it now

those first few weeks are all the things
I didn't say

like how   sometimes loose threads find their way
from pocket to sleeve and I can't explain
how they got there
or what they mean

                            should I say it now

I'm not sure there are words for all this
buttoning and unbuttoning
                            of things

how I counted each part of flesh
as it decamped
                    and my heart was a lime poised
                    for ripening

                            should I say it now

the taste of me soured   sweet

I have overworked it in my head   and still
there are so many things that remain
                                    undone

                            should I say it now

and if you ask me anything
the answer will always be to show you

the silver threads sinking deep into my fingers
holding weight

should I say it now

how in that night I leapt from my body
that instead of falling
I rose

Zelda Chappel

Now, When I Think About Women

I think about Aziz Ansari's Netflix special
where he asked the ladies in the crowd
how many had been followed—not cat-called—
actually followed down the street
by a man, many blocks, and how nearly
half of Madison Square Garden raised
their hands. I was home raising my hand,
thinking of moments in multiple cities,
how it was suddenly time to be scared.
Now, when I think about women,
I think about educated men who ask
if we secretly love being hollered at.
Don't you kind of enjoy the attention?
Isn't it flattering? It is 2017 and my best
friend says: a man in a car pulled up
beside me as I was bicycling, he was
jerking off to me, at me, I froze,
had to force myself to start pedaling
away. Last October, I consoled
my most enthusiastic canvassers: girls
who were chased and assaulted while
trying to get out the vote for the first
female president. Now, when
I think about women, I think about violence
and the threat of violence, how it's like
an alarm inside going from zero to blaring.
The week I moved to New York
a girl my age went for a run.
People said it was her fault for dressing
that way, for taking that path. The article
said there was evidence of a struggle:
that before she died she bit her attacker
so hard her teeth cracked.

Emily Sernaker

Part Four

'Domestic'

No wonder I'm fat

I seemed to be always wearing his hands.
Pinching my earlobe, squeezing
a bit too hard – *why were you talking to him?*
Fingers move under my hair, find the roots,
discreetly pull. *They watch, you know.*
My friends, they tell me everything.

People think nothing of it – just some bloke,
seeing to his lass. *Got your 'andsfull there mate –*
collusion winks across the room, eyes on my breasts
in this tight little dress. Close to my ear – *I could*
have killed you, you know. Taken you up the fields
where nobody would see. I nearly did.

This is what pretty gets you – this, I learn is what comes
of slinking in velour. I used to dance in high heels.
My throat feels like paper under the circle of his grasp.
Tears mark his victory. Loosen his thumbs. *Now then.*
Don't spoil your face. Erection against my thigh,
knee between mine, the bus shelter whines

behind my back. *Don't do it again.*

Jane Burn

In the bedroom

It begins with teasing tongues and gentle hands,
until
your intention shifts:
thrusts roughen, forget to give.
Each stroke forces in dusk
and robs the dawn.
My words fall unheard.

Your weight suffocates
our warm fire – the flame that guards
against the creatures of the night.

Your eyes become a predator's glinting slits.

Kathleen M. Quinlan

Femme

There is a woman inside me whose breasts
have never seen the sun. She is trained
to silence and small tasks, a nun
shorn of her pride, a slave of lists.

She sweeps the floor and wordlessly
washes dishes. The air around her
is perpetual dusk, her hair dank,
nails black, feet foul.

So many hands behind her,
pressing her on; so much to do
to please him, eyes cast down
not in modesty but in fear.

Sarah Mnatzaganian

Button

Persuaded to try medication,
"few side effects, no problem,"

Dr Atul smiles at my husband.
You are just a possession, a car

to service, a house to maintain.
He proudly leads you home,

10 mg of this and that,
and a brand new wife.

Your voice does not matter —
the thickening tongue,

the diminishing libido.
Your body not your own,

your limbs swim in treacle,
your mind, anaesthetised,

your smile, pasted.
The new, improved Wife,

Model 101 — will last
without complaint.

Just press the button.

Jhilmil Breckenridge

Bed

After the sculpture 'Divan Bed'
by Mona Hatoum

It is as if she sleeps on a girder;
fearful of falling, of moving, lest
she give her awakeness away.
Hemmed in by scaffolding, she
has poured herself onto the bed;
posted her limbs in position.
She lies a thousand feet above
the bedroom carpet; her thighs
mottled by steel, arms adorned
with thumbprint bracelets.
Most nights there is a muddling
of limbs, a voiceless barter,
like the scrabble of flyovers.
Her ribs are iron struts, her hips
a hiding place. She has turned
herself inside out. She knows
if he knew, he would crack her
like a fortune cookie.

Beth Somerford

Indoor Sport

You can watch anything you like,
he said. *Except when there's sport on.*
He watched it all, horses, snooker,
rugby, tennis and darts.
Athletes triumphed to his sobs of joy.

A less sporting wife he could not find,
dragged her round London on bicycles,
pedal-crazy, panting to catch up,
braving Marble Arch, Hyde Park,
stomach clenched.

It was his indoor sport she dreaded
when his love of the physical, flexed
his muscles, emptied his eyes, sharpened
his hand skills. Swift upper cut, slap and grab,
his trophies written all over her face.

Rachael Clyne

I might have left

that first time, when
his fingers closed around my neck,
tightened, jerked me to and fro.

He was right.
I needed some sense
shaken into me.

Instead I packed
the incident away, like a forgotten
souvenir of a holiday gone awry.

Perhaps I should have gone when
the glint of blade flashed.
I had a bag by the door, but

no car, no bus, no money.
Only a long snowy road
and a too-thin coat.

Kathleen M. Quinlan

I Don't Know Why

Only god or his grandmother
could love him the way he wants to be loved.
As for me, love sits
fly and spider in my chest.
Not enough he says, I must pay,
pulls open wide lips, slips
the bird a small one, its breast
feathers forked tail,
between teeth, over tongue stuffed,
swallowed warm as a lover.

After the bird the spider the fly,
I got the idea knew the score.
I accepted, ate more, loved less,
wondered why I stayed.
I gave up hope and gentleness,
the pain became hard to ignore.
My ageing, my inertia was paid
in bitterness, after dinner chocolates,
a freezer full of cuts of the best.
I lie beside him sick of the mess.
Perhaps I'll die.

Deborah Alma

Why I didn't marry him

Because he is two men who once loved me
and now lives in the attic. Because he woke me up
with foaming coffee and the cat, and kissed
the top of my right foot before going.
Because he cried in the park when I said I'd leave him
and didn't care if his friends overheard .
Because he had a specific pan for making crepes and burnt
extra butter for flavour. Because he thought my flushed, scaly skin
was cute. The first time we made love his come formed a ring
on my forearm, and he took a picture.
He wasn't afraid of spiders. Because he said
he loved my Maradona hairstyle that time I curled my hair.
He toured 47 apartments with me when I was thinking of moving,
and never complained when I didn't.
Because he invented his own language, and taught me.
Because he had the biggest pimple I'd even seen
on his back and let me pop it. He wrote most of his love
letters on napkins in restaurants. He didn't tell
his cousin that those were my porn tapes. Because
I would have married him if
he were not the one who declawed the cat in secret
and tried to deny it when I saw the stitches.
Or the one who stole my passport and locked me
up in a room for the day, the one
who cut through his stomach to show me what I did to him
when I didn't love him the way he wanted,
who drank too much, then wanted to argue.
If he were not the one who settled his debts by poaching
my father's watch, or who jumped
over the gate and wouldn't leave when I called the police.

Vasiliki Albedo

The Worst Thing

The 17yr old girl sits outside the bathroom
surrounded by the perfume
of things that never get washed.
She is wearing an oversized grey jumper,
she has small hands & ankles
& her thighs are bruised.
She is reading old football mags,
junk mail & copies of the Daily Sport:
the girl loves to read & he has no books.
She reads the words on his posters,
the sleeves of his tape cassettes.
She reads them over again: any words will do.
He is sleeping right next door
on a mattress lay flat on the floor,
she is lonely but she dare not wake him up.
The other boys in the house tried to warn her,
they feel so sorry for her.
But hey, what can they do, they're scared of him too.
It's not a squat but it may as well be,
the landlord overlooks stuff.
Extra lads that live there & the doors smashed in.
He is four years older,
plays messed up games, soppy-tender then he hurts.
The girl is jumped-in-deep-end romantic,
he has black curls & charisma.
She's without words.
He loves to force her, for years she said
he forced her. Her therapist friend said, no
he raped you & that is why you are trembling
& can't get your breath. The girl bites down
on the songbird & spits out feathers.

Ruth Stacey

Something you see in movies

Hotel sheets are waves at rest over her hips –
their scratch softens
where they kiss her skin:
the other girl, the other bed.

Sweat stains the room at 3:54AM
and my comfort is her deepest breaths –
my comfort is the dreams behind her eyelids
of seafoam surrealism, of rolling with a landscape
smudged from oil pastels.

He wants me to wake her, his voice crawls
down my neck to lick between my collarbones.

My focus blurs as threats hula-hoop
my eye sockets, and in my head I'm still stumbling
down a humid street on our midnight sojourn,
childlike, from the bar, hoping to see steam rising

from a manhole – we found one, they exist, it isn't only
something you see in movies. This is New York, real life,
and I refuse to touch the other girl, in the other bed.

My heart beats me backwards to where I am
three years ago: Ohio, crashed out, giggling
stoned under her living room blacklight
that time we all got in a stranger's car;
I borrowed a novel from him
no one else had heard of and woke up
with nothing but a hangover.

My heart xylophones my ribs
as hands pull me back to New York,
back to 3:59AM and through a door
by tangled hair and I can't see if she still sleeps
or how this bathroom is so clean,

but the tiles are cold on my palms
and the tiles are cold on my knees.

This is the only reason he needs me.

don't even try to bite
you just do as you're told

And I do, because
adrenaline beats dopamine,
rock beats scissors
and paper covers rock.

(and I do as I'm told
because he loves me
he says he loves me
this is exactly why he loves me)

I focus on the tiles beneath me
not the burn like a hundred menthol cigarettes
in my throat, the ones I smoked and tossed the butts
into the fireplace at her mother's house
four summers ago.

Later the other girl wakes up refreshed,
asks from the other bed if I'm going with her
to Greenwich Village. No. I can't.

He sleeps. I stare out at the bricks
of the building next door,
close enough to touch if only the window would open.

Kate Garrett

To Hear a Mermaid Sing

Once I nearly drowned and fell in love all in a day.
A goddess saved me from the sea.
Crazed with thirst, horny as hell,
I thought I saw a mermaid and heard her sing.
Her hair made patterns like the waves.
We lay together, panting on a bed of sand.

I've always liked a bed of sand,
a girl who asks for it: whoah lads, my lucky day.
There was magic in the waves.
She swayed in rhythm with the sea.
Ripe, crimson lips opened: she began to sing.
Perhaps I'd died and gone to heaven although hell

is more my scene. And what I got was hell.
True, nothing between us but the sand,
but think about it. Mermaid. Tail. All she could do was sing.
She sang all fucking day.
I was off my head man, rocking with the sea.
At nightfall, hypnotised, I watched her disappear into the waves

and I was gutted. For weeks I scanned those waves,
stood on the shore waiting: it was hell.
I promised I'd change, stop drinking. I slept unshaven by the sea
until one morning dark waters washed her up onto the sand.
Promised I'd marry her that very day
if only she'd sing, if only she'd sing.

Made a fool of me. It wasn't her. She couldn't sing.
Tailless, tongueless, witless slut of the waves.
Not so innocent and pure. Proved it that day.
Got pissed. Had her there and then. Fucking hell.
Called the lads in. Took turns. She was salt and sand.
Fed her vodka. Dunked her in the sea.

I wanted her to drown: she swallowed half the sea.
Rising from the shallows time after time she tried to sing.
No sound but gurgle, spit and splutter - brine and sand.
I walked away but she followed, back turned to the waves
lurching after me towards her new hell.
Alright, I said, come home. Let's give it one more day.

When I'm pissed, I like to watch the sea. Across the waves
some nights I hear a mermaid sing: my private hell.
Face down, breathing wet sand, I dream of her till day.

Jacqueline Saphra

telling secrets (sharifa)

We knew something terrible had happened.

The woman who was our neighbour's sister sobbed.

Our mother made her sweet tea and used the special glasses.

We knew she was different, there was a rhythm to her body.

The woman whispered through lips made into a Sinai
sunset.

Our mother listened with thorny ears, eyes darting,
the door.

We knew secrets were being told and we weren't old enough.

The woman removed her hijab.

Our mother ran to close the curtains.

We knew a neck should not rest so purple on shoulders.

The woman lifted her chin, a world map of maroon borders.

Our mother dabbed antiseptic cotton, we covered our noses.

We knew that smell meant woman flesh woman tears
woman.

The woman, when will my heart be seen for what it is?

Our mother, a wife is the most deluded of people, my dear.

Sabrina Mahfouz

Me Too.

Don't judge her,
unsheathing your sharpened knives,
all the little blades to shuck her naked as an oyster.
You'll find no pearl, only a poison star, set like a bullet.

because the hide-and-secrets grow in the dark,
nestle in eye sockets to be closer to the brain.

Don't watch her,
inventing her face with a clown's palette,
lids garish as Christmas, lips gaudy with lies -
heart skewering the tongue like bitten glass.

because the sudden tannoy in the skull
screams its announcements, rallying demons.

Don't follow her,
venturing closer to the edge than you have ever been
without maps or compass, ignorant of the sun's vigil,
navigating a dark full of missed connections.

because   the endless explanations stretch continents
and she is rowing hard away from the shores of the madwoman.

Lesley Quayle

Domestic

He tried to kill you, strangle you in the bath
but you still want him back.

The belt tightening around your neck
metal buckle cutting into your skin

but you still want him back.
Even when the police come

you in your nightgown
showing the officer the ligature marks on your neck

the welts and bruises on your back.
We can hear the creeping twinge of regret

in your sobbing repertoire
as they place him under arrest.

Later you stand in court
and you declare your love for him

you don't want to see him punished.
He has promised you romance, flowers and a holiday.

That it will *never ever* happen again.
The judge decides on leniency

and suspends the sentence for two years.
You leave with your lover, hand in hand

walking out together in the brilliant sunshine.
I'd like to believe him, for your sake

as I watch you embrace.
The happy couple.

I want to run after you
catch your arm. I want to say, *don't*

men like that don't change
look at my scars, here's the proof.

Rachel Burns

He Loved Me

The first time he loved me
was in the park down the road
from me mam's.
It was a kiss of a different kind,
one that left a bruise
on me cheek.
I love you so much, he said
as he wiped me eyes
with his thumb,
I'll marry you. I'll be yours.
We'll be happy and in love,
forever.
The next time was after we wed,
in a fancy hotel room
in Scarborough.
I wore long sleeves that week.
Even though it was hot,
I was cold.
He loved me a lot, after that.
He said so, every time,
and he cried.
The last time he loved me
was in the kitchen by the door.
I couldn't breathe.
And as the light faded, a thought
so clear it shocked me
to the core.
I didn't want to be loved by him
Anymore.

Cath Campbell

Ending It

Today I didn't send the children to their room
    as knots formed in my belly
    at the sound of your key in the door
I didn't scan for warning signs in your eyes
    on your breath, how you moved,
    cover bruises with make-up and lies
I didn't grill your pork chop just-so
    smooth every lump from your mash
    for you to throw the plate across the room
I didn't bounce off the wall from the fist
    I didn't see coming, feel your hands
    around my throat, lose my breath
I didn't pretend to be asleep as you came up to bed
    hoping you wouldn't drag me out by my hair
    get in with me to do worse
I didn't bleed from my busted nose
    losing our baby which you kicked out of me
    yelling that it wasn't yours.
Last night I put a knife under my pillow.
Tomorrow I will hold my head up.

Jill Abram

Cat

When he beats the kitten to death, I pretend not to see.
It's just a cat, not me, and anyway, he wants
to marry me, even though he knows I am broken.
He's normal. That's what I like. Everything will be better,
and for a while, it is, so long as I behave

but I am not good at being good and one night,
me and the guys stay late at the bar after my shift
and down a few pints, have a laugh, nothing more,
but he doesn't like this and he grabs my hair
and hisses in my ear, *stop behaving*
like a whore, and start behaving
like my wife, and I say *goodnight*
to the guys, who are looking at the floor,
and later on, he says,
it's for your own good, you'll learn
so I don't go back to my shift.
Mostly, I have to stay quiet
and cook him meat, and have sex.
It could be love, if I don't forget.

I ring home each week.
Oh love, best to let it lie,
and I do –
I lie and lie and lie
and when things break,
I clean them up and I stay home
and hide in the loo and write –

and one day the words
walk me right out of the door
and I run with them, but I forget to hide
and soon he comes with a knife
and he's shouting, *Bitch, you can't leave*

but he's drunk and I am sober,
and I get the hell out of there
all the way to the police
who give me a cup of sweet tea
and I tell them about the words,
and the knife, and being quiet
and the policeman tells me
if he does it again, call this number
and I tell him,

if he does it again, I'll be dead.

I remember the kitten then, and the way
its tongue hung out of its crushed head
and I get up, and I walk away
because I'm broken, I know,
but that's ok,
because I'm not a kitten.
I'm a woman
and I'm fucking strong.

Victoria Bennett

Peter and Jane go to the Shops

Jane picks up a lettuce.
Jane likes lettuce. This shop has
the lettuce that Jane likes.

Peter does not like lettuce.
'Let's not buy this lettuce, Jane,' says Peter.
Salad makes Peter cross.
Peter puts the lettuce back.
It is time to go home.

Peter is going away.
Jane helps him pack his suitcase.
'Goodbye Jane,' says Peter.
'Goodbye Peter,' says Jane.
'Go fuck yourself.'

Jane Burn

Body, Remember

Body, remember that night you pretended
it was a film, you had a soundtrack running
through your head, don't lie to me body,
you know what it is. You're keeping it from me,
the stretched white sheets of a bed,
the spinning round of it, the high whining sound
in the head. Body, you remember how it felt,
surely, surely. You're lying to me. Show me
how to recognise the glint in the eye of the dog,
the rabid dog. Remind me, O body, of the way
he moved when he drank, that dangerous silence.
Let me feel how I let my eyes drop, birds falling
from a sky, how my heart was a field, and there
was a dog, loose in the field, it was worrying
the sheep, they were running and then
they were still. O body, let me remember
what it was to have a field in my chest,
O body, let me recognise the dog.

Kim Moore

Part Five

'They can't help it'

Telling Tales

He was the family
friend – the one
she'd been told
to call *Uncle*.

She stopped eating:
if she made herself
small, he might
not notice her.

At last, the truth told
on her frail form: she could
only nod when a teacher
teased out the truth.

Then the other kids
called her *Whore*;
the uncle's wife swore
she was a teller of tall tales.

She was just
a bird-thing
when I met her:
a shadow-slip of a girl

– but she was brave enough
to go on living with the tales
he'd told, over and over,
across her child-body.

Rosie Sandler

Square de la Place Dupleix

Your family weaves you on devotion's loom, rick-racking the bed
LES MURRAY

Inside the sandpit you are playing for your life. Your
bucket and spade that smiled all day long, like family
in your satchel, now work hard. Your material is sand. It weaves
a universe where you are huge, the cellar behind you,
eclipsed by twelve chestnut trees and their pigeon gods. On
and on you burrow, into your sanctuary, devotion's
priest. There are rituals to do, like counting leaves on the sky's loom.
Any lapse and you tumble back into the brain's forks, rick-racking
the minutes for the lock that unclicks, the coffining dark, the
hooded stranger with Papa's voice, the makeshift bed.

Pascale Petit

Irish Twins

attic rain
the backyard swing
off kilter

We share an attic room. In the corner is an old double bed that smells and sags on one side. My side. Late at night I hear my heart beat. Loud. So loud he will hear it. He will think my heart is calling him up the attic stairs. His footsteps are heavy. He smells of old spice and cherry tobacco. My eyes shut tight. I know he is there. I feel his weight. Never on my side. Always on the side she sleeps. When the bed-springs sing their sad song I fly away. Up to the ceiling. My sister is already there. Together we hold hands. Looking down we see our bodies. We are not moving. We are as still as the dead.

Roberta Beary

Attic Room: a Tanka Drama in 4 Acts

Act I

Rough hands rip
a butterfly nightie.
Red blots dot
the white sheet
on my sister's bed.

Act II

Beware all men
father son brother.
They can't help it,
Mother says as she
scrubs my sister's bed.

Act III

Night after night
in their double bed
Mother sleeps the sleep of the dead.
On her pink sleep-mask
white poodles prance.

Act IV

It was a bad dream
but what does it matter,
now he's dead, Mother says
and why does your sister
never visit, never call.

Roberta Beary

Matinee

Twelve years old, two silver quarters singing
in the crease of my palm, the marquee
three streets up, the blue neon letters
washed out to the same color as the sky.
What made me turn my head sideways, toward
the quiet house where he stood naked
between the trees, trembling the shade
of a white-washed duplex, a stranger
looking back at me, holding onto himself
in the sparse light, his eyes opening
and closing, opening and closing.
Why didn't I believe what I saw?
I had seen a man naked before.
I had seen my father undressed, his long white
thighs and the dark scratchy patch between them.
I had seen this, over and over, the pale worm
that grew and bruised up into the air, its
smelly milk, its tiring and slow failing.
I knew what was real and what wasn't.
I knew day from night. And I knew about men,
what they hid beneath their clothes,
so why was I crying? Why was I surprised
to see him there, stroking himself
between the trees? And why was I running?
What was I afraid of? I was twelve. I knew
everything. And it was broad daylight, wasn't it,
pinned to the sky? I had two quarters in my hand,
I could feel them, the ridges along each rim,
the raised faces pressed into my palm.
There were bright cars and sidewalks
and pale green lawns and the movie theater
a single block away, its glittering brick walls
and mirrored doors. I could see it.

I could be there in another minute
if I could only keep running. And I could see
the poster in its glassed case. I could read
the names of the actors and the looks
on their faces. One of them was holding
a handful of roses, I remember how they looked —
so red and so real and so close I thought
I could touch them, I was so sure I could
just reach out and take them into my arms.

Dorianne Laux

My Mother's Dressing Gown

At night she wore a rustling affair
with smoky lining, filmy tree ferns
overlaid with prickly palms –
it was like having a cloud-forest in the room.

Her face was an axed mahogany.
Her hands emerged from emerald sleeves
to meet on the table, talons tensed,
like a puma challenging a tayra.

Her feet – for Maman wore stilettos indoors –
were the stilt roots of fin-trees
and under her gown she wore a moss basque
with bats clinging to her cleavage.

Lianas encased her figure
in the series of corsets
my father bought her
and her legs were snared in mist-net stockings

lit by diamonds of moonlight
filtering through the sub-canopy.
Her pelvis was a bank riddled with burrows
that Papa dug with his nails.

He loved to surprise her by inventing
new raids on her nests.
She was a smoulder of leaves
in the lee of a bushfire, flat

under the steamrolling man who owned her.
From my cot, I heard cries
only a cornered peccary would make.
I'd wake screaming from night terrors,

then Maman would come, her robe alight,
but Papa would order her back to bed.
And then there'd be nothing
between me and my father.

Pascale Petit

Five Years

My five years were the inverse of Bowie's.
Earth was fine, but I was dying.
And the thing that I think you should know is
I was dying I was dying I was dying.

I went to school went home and died.
Got up in the dark went back and died.
I locked the bathroom, cut my hair off, died.
Shaved the last sad tufts, walked out, and died.

Was kissed by boys and froze, then died.
Got pissed and stoned, got caught
And went to court, then died.
Turned down a bag of skag, survived: still died.

Was perved at in the papers, died.
Escaped to haunted pavements, died.
Had several breakdowns pre-eighteen
and still perfected dying in between.

I daily died and died and died and died and
died and died and died and died and died and
then he died
and then I lived.

That's all there is.

Claire Leavey

Killing Me Softly

The inmates of the younger houses ate
in the large campus cafeteria.
Older children progressively took their
meals in their cottages, learning to cook
so that, the theory went, they could function
in the world after their graduation.
By the time I reached that phase there were padlocks
on all the cabinet doors. In Brophy,
the cottage where the newest orphans were
stashed to adjust, the only in-house
food consisted of Sisco-company
off-brand rice crispy treats and nacho chips.
Sisco is a major supplier to
prisons and every morsel we ate came
either from the on-campus farm or their
warehouses. Every evening we'd gather
outside of the dark, stone-walled living-room
(the only part of the house that did not
smell like industrial cleaners — the room
the rarely-visiting parents saw) and
flock onto the back porch, into the shade
of a sprawling, spindle-limbed live-oak. Moss
flapped against the roof when the wind blew. Red
mites rained down to burrow in our naked
pores. We stood in a circle and held hands,
bowing our heads for our mandatory
prayers. One day, when it was Fallon's turn, she
squeezed my hand (my hymen-blood still drying,
dark, beneath her nails) and said, 'Dear Lord, please
help Bethany to be less stupid, less
bad.' My eyes snapped open and she smirked, 'Help
her to listen to our House-Mother and
her Student Supervisor. Lord, make her
be better. Let her be quiet and good.' I
could hear a radio playing somewhere,

at a distance; it was something I knew.
The Fugees, singing the song I was raped
to. I felt something hard and cold slide into
my guts. The world wavered, and then (praise God)
I felt nothing at all. Fallon traced her
red nail across the blue veins in my wrist.
Dinner that night was fried chicken, soggy
and cold along the pinkish bone. Dessert
was a Snickers ice-cream bar. I held it
in my lap until the vanilla warmed.
I sucked the sweet slurry heart from the milk
chocolate shell, pretending
all the time that I was pithing something else.

Bethany W Pope

Fallon

You were wounded, demented, a bad little girl,
Grinning as you slid your fingers into me.
I never thought I'd catch myself praying for your soul
After you told me that, now, I could never be loved. My small
Body was a canvass for your vengeance;
You were wounded, demented, a bad little girl
Still angry at your mommy for selling you to tall,
Grown men whose cocks (you said) tasted like pee.
I never thought I'd catch myself praying for your soul
When, years later, you let your filthy orange urine fall
Into my mouth as you used your woven belt to choke me.
You were wounded, demented, a bad little girl,
And I was unsurprised when I learned you'd landed in jail,
Though the crime they nailed you for was unrelated to rape.
I never thought I'd catch myself praying for your soul,
When I spent the night vomiting after giving my all
Attempting to make love to the man that I married, but this is true:
You were wounded, demented, a sad little girl
And I just caught myself praying for your soul.

Bethany W Pope

What you do when your child is born of rape

You make sure you love her more
than a longed-for child.
You search her genes for traces;
thank god her hair is dark, not fair.

You leapfrog thoughts to explain
why you're not with her father.
You spit the word *father*
because he doesn't deserve it.

She asks what he's like. You squint
to find good things to plonk on an altar
to an angry god. You realise that
you are the angry god.

You fret over the havoc
your rage created - she grew
in an indignant womb.
You startle when she startles.

You hope when she's a teenager
she won't wear it like a badge.
If you taught her not to trust,
it would be wrong.

You build her self-esteem
as a monument to your overcoming.
You find one hundred ways to teach her
not to take what isn't hers.

Louisa Campbell

What they Cannot Measure

Evidence suggests
that a stressed mother
will pass unwise hormones
to the foetus, that cortisol
and adrenalin will directly
flow to the unborn child.

These studies entered my blood,
revved up the guilt organ, sent bile
and lactic acid on the rampage.

Sometimes I wish I'd never pressed charges,
never been believed (finally) so that
days in court would never have happened

and I'd have been at home making a belly
cast, eating pickles, having odd dreams &
defending myself against stretch marks;

but it's known in the quiet of my bones
that when the house timbers creak,
they speak of the forest.

I couldn't have been looking forward
to your first words knowing
I'd held mine back.

clare e. potter

The Silence of Gassed Cats

Though you're gone, your silence hangs about,
the terse sighs, the tight lips, sucked breath.
They're sarcastic, noiseless tones that reach me
in the mouths of my son and brothers (your
dynastic line of wrecked kings) while my sister
and I say nothing of the flat smile that silenced
your abuse. You bent our innocence,
wrung our hearts – made feelings obtuse.

Why, despite your parents' law - heft
that denied a young tongue and ruled their boy
watch his pet cat get gassed in a vet's glass jar -
did you not see you had a choice?

Your childhood makes me cry, but not for you.
You didn't have to gas your children, too.

Vicky Hampton

Without Narcissus

The lack of his blindness shocks the silver water
black. Your palm's slap against its surface is looped silence:
bare shoulders with their heron stoop, the wet ropes
of your hair, the empty water and the silent throats of lilies. *Speak.*

Over the water the red rock leans and watches.
Your nails like fish-scales break against the shadow
of its noon, and the silence. *Speak.*

Even the fish have voices, even the rough
hush of the trees, even the birds. You press your body
to the dark-loomed sediment, learn the syllables
of its unspeech. *Speak.*

Birds watch you writing the mangled sign of your name

hair strung across the mats of cress, your lips
kissed against the petals of the lilies. You can speak
their silence back to them so well, so well.

Rhiannon Hooson

Part Six

'I Said I Was the Proof'

Still guilty

Years ago, I saw a stranger at the hotel bar,
        a little girl between his knees.
A latter-day James Cagney, cocky, plump hand
slung too heavy over childish shoulder,
                        pensively fondling
        a prepubescent breast.
        He looked me straight in the eye.
I stared at him, and he knew that I knew,
                        and I wondered what to say
when doting family were gathered round him
like a painting. Patriarch surrounded by his heirs.
        So, I kept hoping, in that awkward,
        British way, that he'd give up,
that I would shame him with my weighty gaze,
                        and he kept catching my eye
and smiling.   On the way home, I said
Did you see that?
                        I should have done something.

Kathy Gee

Keynote Speech

If you want politically correct
you're in the wrong place.
You know what he's like –
brash, self-indulgent, in yer face.
His arrogance is refreshing,
his challenge to convention
a wake-up call, a kick in the butt.
So you're sitting there, bowling along
to the rhythms of his expletives,
his hectoring tirades.
And then he acts out this story:
a woman standing up to him,
his hand raised, 'Shut up bitch',
the motion of striking.
The laughter is uncomfortable
but in the moment
when you could have objected
you imagine him turning towards you,
sneering, calling you bourgeois.
So you sit tight, diminished
by your failure to stand up,
to be counted.

Angi Holden

'I Said I Was the Proof'

Rose McGowen

no-one believed her
he'd done this
and this surprised her
men had been doing this
since she grew breasts
but not all men
though some men seemed to care
more about this no not all men
than all women
so that what she's saying
you couldn't always tell
some women knew
but no-one believed them
that face this skirt those breasts
knowing what men are like
not just some men
sometimes it was just one man
saying you think I'd do this with that
some men and some women
saying it's not great this
but at least it's not
as though this meant they believed her
even if it wasn't as bad or as often
as she said and they said
you can stop can you stop
and then that man
to some women many women
and some told men
but didn't make a fuss
and others asked why these women
should have could have
their bodies knew the truth

bodies were proof
but bodies need a voice
and when the women all the women
who had this or that
by this man or other men
tried to
how hard it was
when no-one listened
how shameful
no-one believed them

Emma Simon

Too close

She works with us in Social Care;
all plugged into our headsets,
referrals from the public, bad
things that might've happened.

Lucky it's chilly – she can cover up:
polo-necks, long sleeves. Her face
is harder – no one should have to
look at that sort of thing.

We are diligent at our screens
as she moves amongst us
to the photocopier, to the files,
to the water cooler, too close.

We say nothing. We don't say;
she must've known he was…
put herself at risk… still single….

We don't say it when she's there.

Holly Magill

Stuck

You say up front, it's not PC, but still,
you're going to tell it anyway, because we
are listening and, what the heck, it's Friday.

So; this joke's an opportunist in a lift
that's stuck. Implied are cipher women
getting knocked about, knocked out,

knocked up, but they're not real,
just women-in-a-joke, and they don't feel
a steel wall slam into their cheek,

the fumbling of a beery, bristly bloke
who's rucking up their skirts, and then
the shame, the hurt. They don't react;

they're disbelief, suspended between floors,
and just how rapey is it? As we fall
towards the punchline, down the shaft,

I just can't answer back; in this tight spot
I sense that lurch and drop. I'm pressed against
these sliding doors that closed and will not open.

Judi Sutherland

Fireman's lift

Do you know that dangerous state
when you're too far gone to work out
if the boy chatting you up
is as wasted as you are,
even if you could rouse yourself to care?

I remember watching a bloke
carry a girl through a club
like he was a hero.
Limp. Her arse neat in a tight skirt.
No one doing anything about it.

Ramona Herdman

Consent

She drags it out of me
with vodka and shouting;
How fucking dare he!
The state of your face…

Tears only have her snarling:
I am so tired – I cannot soothe her,
make it better.

Give me his address –
I'll sort him out for you.

Knuckles bulge white as she wrings
the stem of her glass – always
stronger than me.

I edge back, coil what's broken
further into the sofa,
away, away, away.

I'll kill him, I swear:
no one touches my friend.

The door nearly off its hinges,
she leaves to serve my vengeance;
doesn't ask what I want.

Holly Magill

Bejantine

Students, all women in our freshest years,
we settled on landings with mugs of tea,
and, late into the night as *Sweet Baby James*
floated up the stairwell, we gossiped, fell out,
time-shared bedrooms for lover trysts,
never thought to lock our doors.

Then she disappeared,
that girl of the fiery perm and Scouser sound.
We wondered in the silence.
Her space filled over
like a river after extreme rainfall.

I imagined her walking back after drinks at the Union,
in her silk halter neck and corduroy flares,
humming Joni Mitchell in her head,
caught in a clutch, dragged into a flowerbed,
calling for her Mum.

We stopped walking alone.
We avoided the garden. Then we forgot.

Maggie Mackay

Signals

I should've said *get up and leave*,
but I didn't because you'd brought me
a fucking mix tape, and it fucking had
SLINT on it. I fucking love SLINT.

I tried spelling *STOP* in Braille on your back,
like on the square buttons you can stroke
during bus journeys – the kind that allow you
to halt the ride and jump off.

The pain stopped me in my tracks,
and by the time I recovered my voice
to let out a whimper, tears were rolling
down my face like shooting stars.

I wasn't mad when you said you misread
the signals. Apparently I did something
that was an invitation for you to take
something from me without permission.

I turned my back on you,
rescued the needle from the far end
of the player, back to the record,
and played *True Love Waits*
on repeat through the night.

Alicia Fernández

The Library of Broken People

is catalogued by injury: the fractured;
the ruined from hunger; the raped;

the hammered shut. Some are clumped
together as "lost souls"; only the librarian

can retrieve those. There's no ABC to damage,
they litter the alphabet ad hoc. If you browse

the catalogue they gift their injuries, lay
themselves flat. Last week two girls displayed

their abdomens to a first-year student □
bickered over abuse, spoke of neglect,

said life's an unworkable toy. Other victims
are quieter, don't talk so much, even when

the library's shut. They drop to the back
of an index, all seal pup eyed, bones skittering

at the slightest flex. I survive amongst them,
wear a long jumper, drag sleeves down wrists.

Abegail Morley

Why did I say nothing?

Because I was young and ignorant and I couldn't believe what he was
doing and we were having a conversation for goodness sake on the bus
from Lairg in the middle of the afternoon

and because I was brought up to be polite and I couldn't think of the right
thing to say and I didn't want to make a scene and of course he would
have denied it anyway

and because I was embarrassed and because I was ashamed and because
I was scared and a long way from home and out of my depth and I didn't
even have a word for

so I pretended it wasn't happening and afterwards I tried to forget and I
never told anyone and who would believe such a thing could happen on
a bus in broad daylight?

Ama Bolton

#metoo, sings a millennial

after Langston Hughes

I too have been harassed, assaulted even.
I am the quieter daughter.
The one who doesn't want to think of it in labels.

The kind who sees people, sees situations,
sees how in a moment everything and nothing changes.
I am the 37-year-old woman whose index fingers

can't bring themselves to press 6 keys.
As if they would twist their way around a can of words
that would come spilling out all over the screen.

And who would scoop them up and sort them into 280 powerful
characters for me. And where is the filter to convey to the people
the way my body did not feel from the ceiling, looking down.

Natalie Rees

Reunion

It never crossed my mind that you had
twenty years of wanting me
rattling around your brain or that
you would take the chance to claim me

when we sat on that bed and joked
about the old days, lectures,
student drinking games, bunking
off seminars and flunking grades,

that you would want to plant
your skull & crossbones in this trusting
territory of a mate, drinking buddy, shoulder
cried on.
                    I cried, when you held my wrists,

when you looked at me like I was a blow-up
doll, *a tease, a prick tease, you're a*
                    fucking prick tease.
I cried, shut my eyes and my mouth disappeared.

No.
        Get off me.
                            I said,
No.

The next morning, you left before I woke,
slipped from my emptied body
and later onto Facebook, telling everyone
what a great night it was, *must do it again soon,*

and I clicked Like
because I didn't know what to do,
and all our Friends would wonder why I didn't
post anything for them to share.

Sarah Miles

Part Seven

'make for the light'

Spunk

after Jacob Epstein's *Adam*

His cock hangs at half mast; it's primed to score:
rising, monstrous; nothing like those bland
and flaccid members in rooms 3 and 4.
Drunk on lust, pumped up with blood, he stands
broad on his plinth and howls for cunt. Who'd dare
to leave that call unanswered? This is where
we find the source: that first, primeval sin:
he forced an opening, she let him in.

Later they wrote *she asked for it* - her pink,
seductive flesh, the bruise and not the kiss.
You ask who wrote those books: who do you think?
Would you, with longing, spread your legs for *this*,
bear more like him? It seems so far to fall.
Must this man be the father of us all?

Jacqueline Saphra

We too

We are Eve, we are forked
tongue, we are the silky,
sex-scent of petrol, slippery
on your fingers, the fizzing*hiss*
crack as you strike a match.
We are nails scratching
harder, fuck
me
harder on black velvet. We
are "QUEEN" shouted from
scaffold-smashed rubble. We
are that burning fire emoji,
ammonia's acrid stink. In
our boxing ring we wear split-
lip rust – and
our hands bleed iron.
We are extra heavy flow, we
pour out of ourselves, and we
wash away.

You put your hands up our skirts as
we walk through Leicester Square,
grab our breasts in the back of taxis,
stand too close to us on the tube,
pressed against our bottoms.
You whistle as we push buggies
to nursery, as we run, hot sweat
metal in the park.
Alright, darlin'? Fucking bitch –
fucking cold, fucking frigid bitch.
We are tetanus kisses
– shout "fire",nobody comes
if you shout "rape" –

and we are our mothers' cries.
We are candles and oval faces, a
ghost bike, tied to a lamp-post.
What a shame. Wasn't she pretty?
We explode with our blue skin,
and we are coming for you.
We too.

Victoria Richards

Pinning Photographs

I want to stick a pin
right where your heart would be

I want to shove a pin
in your eye
so you can see how it feels

I want to push a pin
through the paper
and hit the corkboard underneath

I want you pinned
right where I can see you

Lisa Oliver

The Inequity of Goats

Mama learned me scarper brittle edges,
trip-trap soft on clefties.

Papa learned me lean - lean in to rock,
follow, follow, follow.

Me learn nifty - sidestep cracks and rifties.
Me learn no graze bitter-bitter trampled raze,

me reach-reach high, browse ledges,
learn munch. Me grow little nubs, grow brave,

grow life, learn give-give-bend, earn reach,
teach kids four-feet-fend.

Then come Gruffs - bristle me with horn,
chests out-puff, beards strokey-strokey,

blah-blah me glassy-eyed.
Blather-blather richer pasture, wide-wide opens.

Tells of green blades stropped on leathery tongue,
the sweet-suck-scent of heathery highs.

Tells how Gruff get all good things if him strong.
If him stretch, him reach-reach sky.

Me blurt - them look me slit, narrow-narrow.
'No-no,' them wags. 'No reach for Nounous,

them's broody-breeds, made to follow.
Gruffs learned me pain to marrow,

caused me blart so hard me split sides,
spill out innards, bawl out eyes. So hard me sick-up heart.

~   ~   ~   ~

It looked pathetic lying there, pooled in offal and hair.
I wrapped it in the tatters of my kiddy-hide,

left it to harden beside the shucked off corns of hoofs,
the dazed gaze of rolling eyes.

I grew a thicker skin, got more guts,
clearer vision. Sharpened the points of my horns.

Stella Wulf

Asylum*

I ran like a rat in the night, from men's hands
and unspeakable things. An owl beat
its wings in my chest. I swam rivers,
hid in bushes, wept for my lost child, family.
I thanked God for the miracle of an aeroplane ticket.

In your wet country, faces with no pity,
no money, no work. Nobody to tell us
how to walk minefields of laws not explained,
how to avoid the teeth of lazy, fat crocodiles
who make money sending us back.
How can we tell our shame to men
who do not believe us, who detain us,
who do the same as those we fled from?

But we little rats found one other
grew instead into a pride of lionesses
learned to roar stories that choked us
and claim the right to stay. No longer sorry
for ourselves, together we make asylum
mean what it really means. We still thank God.

Rachael Clyne

*tales from the All African Women's Group: a self-help group of Asylum Seek-
ers in E. London, who are powerful advocates for each other. We have held re-
treats for them in Glastonbury, offering respite and a glimpse of green.'

On My Walk this Morning

On my walk this morning I saw
a female blackbird, her dun
feathers a match to the ground
between the grass.

I saw a sign post drunk in a hedge.
I saw the roots of the hawthorn
strangely exposed, tangled and grasping.

On my walk this morning I crushed the heads
of chick weed and smelled the lemon
scent on my fingers. I watched the corn ripen.

I lifted my face to the sun
and closed my eyes and smelled lavender
and clover.

On my walk this morning a man pulled
a white van up next to me and said
something about a spare mattress
from a shop that had closed in York. He said

he was delivering one to a farm up the road,
but thought he'd ask the locals if
they wanted the other. I said no.
Thanks.
                    And my first thought was: rapist.

On my walk this morning I saw all the things
I'm supposed to see, and the things
that are behind the scenes.

Wendy Pratt

Aftermath

Drain pipes are clogged. Never used to happen. Rats have moved in
to the gutters and built nests on the grate. There is no physical
pain. I feel the clogged-upness. Rain can't
flow through. It's always dark
in here. I didn't know
this would echo
for years.

When I moved house, eventually & at last, a welcome
finality, I wasn't sure what
to do exactly or how
things would play out.

I was surprised when he kept bringing me
fresh flowers. Lavender cleansed the air. Daisies returned
innocence. Sage, burnt at both ends, kept the rats
at bay. Rose petals – a reminder of the existence
of gentleness somewhere in the world.
Cinnamon & orange candles ignited
new beginnings.

Sometimes the hearth receives only
damp logs. Smoke billows throughout
the belly of the house. I breathe in
the grey death
it stays in my bones & veins
for days.

On dark moon nights
I remember
to light the candles.

Bethany Rivers

Candlewick

I stole
it from my mother's house.
I love
the way it blankets the busyness of my room –
it settles,
soft as a fall of snow.
Smooth
under palms, my fingers plough its fluted tactility,
burrow out
smells of lavender stored in folds, since I last
unpegged
its ghost from the fanning line. The airing cupboard
treasures
its bundle – I un-shroud the parcel, humble, devout.
Unveiled
on special days, at times when the spreading of it
makes me
think of weddings – of its waiting to be
soiled
by breaking blood. A breeze
through
the open window huffs the fringed edge,
like a veil
of dithering wings. The woollen lines press softly
in my flesh
and I swallow a pinch of pain at the sight of it.
Hold
the bedside flame in my eyes for a while, then blow
into darkness.

Jane Burn

When I Open

When I open my ribs a dragon flies out
and when I open my mouth a sheep trots out
and when I open my eyes silverfish crawl out
and make for a place that's not mine.

When I open my fists two skylarks fly out
and when I open my legs a horse gallops out
and when I open my heart a wolf slinks out
and watches from beneath the trees.

When I open my arms a hare jumps out
and when I show you my wrists a shadow
cries out and when I fall to my knees
a tiger slips out and will not answer to me.

Now that the tree that grew in my chest
has pulled up its roots and left, now that I'm open
and the sky has come in and left me with nothing
but space, now that I'm ready to lie like a cross

and wait for the ghost of him to float clear away,
will my wild things come back, will the horse
of my legs and the dragon of my ribs,
and the gentle sheep which lived in my throat

like a breath of mist and the silverfish
of my eyes and the skylarks of my hands
and the wolf of my heart, will they all come back
and live here again, now that he's left,

now I've said the word whisper it rape
now I've said the word whisper it shame
will my true ones, my wild, my truth,
will my wild come back to me again?

Kim Moore

Nightingale

They say arnica will heal bruises, trauma,
wounds– too little, too late, too far for you,
perched high above mangled tree roots.
You nestle in thorns, in sheet-like briars.
Feathered in subdued browns,
you have been put in your place, and muted.

But try. Hear other tongues rise up
in Edinburgh's Meadows,
in Delhi's fume-choked traffic,
in disbelieving Hampshire,
in ISIS slave auctions at Raqqa.
Make another tongue rise up in you
and hew rough sounds of truth,
tee-rew, tee-rew, jug, jug.

Georgi Gill

You Will Never Be Anyone Else

so you – yes you,
with your warts and wings
will just have to do.

Acceptance is your food
and shelter without which
you are brushwood

for any foul wind
that cares to blow. Stop
using the poison

bottle labelled *'Drink me'*
it's not OK.
It's that simple,

I didn't say easy.

Rachael Clyne

Defence Mechanisms

If I didn't have a body
I couldn't be raped

– like my childhood friend,
assaulted by the sweetshop owner

or my fellow student, years later,
attacked by the night-bus driver.

So I draped my frame in shapeless
clothes, cloaked it in bravado,

wore a mask of sarcasm
and dreamed myself neuter.

But one brave man came tapping
on the shell of my disguise,

his safe embrace a pledge
that not all men are rapists,
not all encounters damaged.

I don slim dresses now,
short skirts, high heels.

But I stay away from
sweet shops and night buses,

avoid eye contact with strangers,
still fence with words.

Rosie Sandler

#Not him

He did not pinch her arse or follow her slowly in his car.
He did not push her up against the unforgiving wall,
and stick his circling tongue deep down her choking throat.
He did not take advantage of her when she cried and shared
she thought her guy was staying late at work and telling lies.
#Not him

He would never say her dress was cut too low, or find fault
in the way she'd styled her hair. He would never comment
on the extra pounds, the growing darkness round her ageing eyes.
He would never mock her tendency to cook the make-do meals
she'd cooked the weeks, the months, the years before.
#Not him

He couldn't bring himself to laugh at sexist jokes in work
or down the pub. He couldn't bear to be the man that other
men felt he should be, the footie-loving, poetry-shunning,
cave man of a bloke. He couldn't find it in himself to
hide his love, his tears, his fear of spiders and of death.
#Not him

He's not alone of course,

#Me too said his son.

Pat Edwards

Freeing the sources of light

Make friends with the light.
It's been years
since you watched summer turn bad,

felt warm grass chafe your bare legs
and his old man's fingers
trespass beneath the dress

you never wore again.
That hot summer
you dashed to your childhood garden

but the sun glared,
music buzzed from the wireless,
stung a secret place the Everlys

and Elvis called *heart*:
always tender, *baby*,
always *untrue*.

And summers afterward
echoed bus rides to city parks
where he kissed your mouth,

fondled your arms.
The sun blurred, twinned
into headlamps,

pinned shadows on the wall-
but it was decades ago.
Welcome the light,

you don't need a sky's worth,
just a lodestar for the journey.
White roses in a glass vase,

candle-flame at dusk and the moon
in winter carrying
its bowl of borrowed sun.

Sheila Jacob

Butterfly

So, you leave the skins clinging
to the lane's camber,
a plague of caterpillars
picked from ragwort along the railway
and squished
to see the juice squirt,

and you drop, fallen angel,
through the lane door
to the garden
and the vets under the coal shed,
mending croaking frogs,
a bird the cat broke.

There are worse ways to learn
how life works,
the dark mechanics of the heart –
in the house
things are made
unbendingly black and white.

Later, you'll emerge
from the front door stretching
your wings on a red and yellow bicycle.
Forever
flying down the road
without stabilizers.

Vicky Hampton

Wildwood

It's time to leave this house

Glancing up as I cut the grass
I see three apples, green in leaves,
the first-ever crop on the tree I grew
from the seed of the final fruit
picked in my grandmother's garden

I'll watch them swell and ripen
take the pips with me when I go,
plant a tree that might not blossom
in the years that are left

There are millions of seeds in pots and jam jars,
spilling from mouths of paper bags
one for each minute of each day lost,
copses, forests, wildwood
falling through my fingers

I reach for the hands of my children, my sisters,
our dormant stories stir in earth
make for the light

Deborah Harvey

#MeToo

When you first got breasts, aged twelve. The winks,
the *nice tits (it's a compliment)*, the *show us your
bra*. How far is too far? That man in Oxford Street
who pushed you against a wall *for a feel*. No big
deal. He liked the look of you, that's all. Every blown
kiss and catcall – a compliment. The one who wanked
at you in an Islington park – it wasn't even dark, broad
daylight, but he was so blatant. The colleagues wanting
to take you for a drink – *just one drink – we'll all think
you're a lesbian if you don't*. That time in someone's
car. The corridor squeeze, the accidentally brushed breasts,
the ease with which they do it. That date where the kissing
went too far, and you couldn't make it stop – how he
surprised you, the strength of him, his knee rising between
your thighs, too determined to be shaken off, and you
didn't feel entitled to name it rape because he didn't hit
you, but the shame, to be so easily caught, the *my fault
my fault* mantra you recited into your pillow for years.
Enough tears. Enough silence. It was all of us but we
never knew. Sisters, take my hands, we can say it together:

    me too

            me too

                    me too.

Sarah Doyle

This poem is for you

carrying a bale of warm towels
house low lit, quiet

a great silence recently
come to my heart

a long quiet such as one might
find buried in a seam of coal

I think of your darkness
far away, weightless as a crane fly.

On the stairs, I stop half-way
and remember

as every so often I must do
of being scattered

in the tread of your boot. Of women
gathering me in boat arms

attending there, as one dawn
gave way to another, until I was strong.

I remember and though my
front is soft as lawn, as milk

a buried lesson is diamond
in my bones and seems to shine.

Roz Goddard

Spartaca

in the room/ in the street/ on the stair/ where some men make free
in plain sight or in secret as if we were sweetmeat/ to dip
fingers in and then forget – it is the being alone
afterwards that numbs and maims, utterly
alone in the silence of it/ where shame creeps in/
stuns dead/ but now we rise, all women
fondled and hurt and licked in acid jokery and in hate,
pets, sweethearts, loves, darlings, humourless bitches –
we stand together, each one a Spartaca
no longer silent or alone: each voice stronger,
massing, alive, a wild murmuration
of me too/ me too/ me too

Pippa Little

*Spartacus was a rebel slave hunted down by the Romans to be crucified.
Asked to identify himself by soldiers, everyone in the crowd around him
stepped forward and said 'I am Spartacus'.*

Acknowledgments

I am deeply grateful to all of the poets who have donated poems to this project, in support of the book, and to help raise funds for Women's Aid: both to the wonderful poets published here and the many whose work did not quite make it between the covers because of lack of space. Some of these poems are published online and can be found courtesy of Vik Bennett at www.wildwomenpress.com

Jess Phillips - for everything you have done on behalf of women both at Women's Aid and now in parliament - and then taking the time in an extraordinarily busy life to write our foreword - the words 'thank you' aren't enough - but thank you x

My special thanks to Vik Bennett of *Wild Women Press* without whose encouragement this book would never have happened.

A huge thank you for the new artwork, to Sandra Salter and Jessamy Hawke, for the cover & chapter heading illustrations, which were gifts to the book.

Thanks to lovely publisher, and friend, Nadia Kingsley of *Fair Acre Press* for all her bloody enthusiasm and spirit, often as we swum up and down together in Oswestry swimming pool and to her partner Gian for lovely lunches afterwards.

My especial thanks to Keele University's Faculty of Humanities and Social Sciences for their financial support which has made all the difference to the project.

Thank you to wonderful Ana McLaughlin @AnaBooks for publicity and promotion advice and for supporting the project on social media and elsewhere and asking me awkward questions.

Finally for my partner James Sheard who has been utterly and always one of the very best of men and who has seen at close hand the awful damage wreaked by sexual assault on someone he loved; and who has suffered from it too. Thank you Jim for all of your help and belief in this book and for your love.

The editor and publisher gratefully acknowledge permission to reprint copyright material in this book as follows:

Jill Abram – *Ending It*, first published in *Well Versed* (The Morning Star, 13th July 2017)

Roberta Beary – *Irish Twins*, from *Contemporary Haibun Vol. 14* (Red Moon Press, 2015) & *Attic Room: a Tanka Drama in 4 Acts*, first published in *Cultural Weekly* (14 Dec 2017)

Kaddy Benyan – *Undone*, first published on *Granta Online* (2012) & then in *Milk Fever* (Salt, 2012)

Cath Campbell – *He Loved Me*, first published by *I Am Not A Silent Poet* (May 2016)

Zelda Chappel – *Skinned*, first published in *The Girl in the Dog-tooth Coat* (Bare Fiction Press, 2015)

Elisabeth Sennitt Clough – *Fidget*, first published in *Glass* (Paper Swans Press, 2016)

Rachael Clyne – *Indoor Sport*, first published in *Domestic Cherry* & *You Will Never Be Anyone Else*, first published in *Obsessed with Pipework*.

Sarah Doyle – *#MeToo*, first published in *Well Versed* (The Morning Star, 19th October 2017)

Pat Edwards - #Not him, published in *Prole 24*

Kate Garrett – *Something you see in movies*, first published in *The Black Light Engine Room Literary Magazine* & then in the pamphlet *You've never seen a doomsday like it* (Indigo Dreams, 2017)

Deborah Harvey – *Wildwood*, first published in *Breadcrumbs* (Indigo Dreams, 2016)

Rhiannon Hooson – *Without Narcissus*, first published in *The Other City* (Seren, 2016)

Helen Ivory – *Scold's Bridle*, and *Dissecting Venus*, both published in *The Anatomical Venus* (Bloodaxe Books, 2019)

Sally Jenkinson – *Nervous*, & *Giantess*, were first published in *Boys* (Burning Eye Books, 2016)

Dorianne Laux – *Matinee*, first published in *What We Carry* (BOA Editions, 1994)

Liz Lefroy – *An Ancient Settlement*, first published on *Ink, Sweat and Tears* website

Mandy Macdonald – *scathless*, first published in *Poetry Scotland* (Dec 2013)

Maggie Mackay – *Bejantine*, first published in *Riggwelter Issue#3* (Nov 2017)

Kim Moore – *I Have Been a Long Time Without Thinking*, & *When I Open*, were first published in *The North* & *Body, Remember,* from *The Art of Falling* (Seren, 2017)

Abegail Morley – *The Library of Broken People*, first published in *Biot Vol. 1*

Katrina Naomi – *The Bicycle*, first published in *The Way the Crocodile Taught Me* (Seren, 2016) & *The Forward Prize anthology 2017*

Pascale Petit – *Square de la Place Dupleix*, and *My Mother's Dressing Gown*, were first published in *Mama Amazonica* (Bloodaxe, 2017)

clare e. potter – *Between Us*, first published in the *Pikeville Review, Kentucky*

Lesley Quayle – *Me Too*, first published in *I Am Not A Silent Poet*

Kathleen M. Quinlan – *In the Bedroom*, first published in *From We to I* (Cinnamon Press, 2015) & *I Might Have Left,* first published in *150 Poems for Human Rights* (University of London, 2013)

Jacqueline Saphra – *Spunk*, first published in *Binders Full of Women*, a chapbook edited by Sophie Mayer and Sarah Crewe, then subsequently in *All My Mad Mothers* (Nine Arches Press, 2017)

Emily Sernaker – *Now, When I Think About Women*, first published on *Poets Respond* (October 22 2017)

Angela Topping – *Sometime Before Myra*, first published in The Cheshire Prize Anthology *Crossings Over* (Chester University Press, 2017)

Stella Wulf – *After Eden*, first published by *Three Drops* 2017 & *The Inequity of Goats*, first published by Nine Arches Press in *The Very Best of 52*, under the title *Giving Up the Goat*.

All profits from the book will be donated to Women's Aid

To read more about the necessary work that they do visit their website www.womensaid.org.uk, and their free online book:
The Survivor's Handbook
©Copyright Women's Aid Federation of England 2005 all rights reserved. Revised Jun 2009.

Scottish Women's Aid   sdafmh.org.uk/
Freephone 0800 027 1234

24 hr National Domestic Violence Helpline
(Run in partnership between Women's Aid and Refuge)
Freephone 0808 2000 247

Refuge at www.refuge.org.uk/

Rape Crisis England & Wales rapecrisis.org.uk/
Freephone 0808 802 9999

Rape Crisis Scotland www.rapecrisisscotland.org.uk/
Freephone 0808 801 0302

New Pathways: Rape Crisis and Sexual Abuse Support Services in Wales:
www.newpathways.org.uk/
01685 379 310

Lightning Source UK Ltd.
Milton Keynes UK
UKHW02f0224060318
318968UK00008B/53/P